The Key to Happiness

Leading a Fulfilling Life

Written by:-

HUGO HUYER

ISBN: 9798366913164

DEDICATION

This project is dedicated to Almighty GOD who in His infinite mercy gave me all the wisdom and strength required to start and complete this project successfully.

Table of contents

Introduction

The Key to Happiness and Leading a Fulfilling Life

For every person, happiness looks different. It could be being content with who you are, having a solid group of friends who are willing to accept you, or having the ability to follow your wildest aspirations.

No matter how you define true happiness, a happier, more contented existence is attainable. You can get there by making a few adjustments to your daily routines.

If you have ever wondered how to be happy with yourself, understand that habits and how you look at life play a significant role. No one can be happy all the time, but one can try and learn to be.

The following are some scientifically proven ways one can be happy in life. Remember that everyone's happiness and method for being happy slightly differ. You'll discover what method works for you with time and effort.

If I ask you "what is happiness?", then what would your answer be? It's probably difficult to come up with a simple answer. Yet, here you are, looking for a key to happiness and how to lead a fulfilling life.

The truth is that **a universal key to happiness is a myth.**

That doesn't mean that you should stop looking for yours right now, it only means that you need to be careful when reading articles about "a key to happiness". The universal key to happiness is non-existent because happiness is one of the most difficult things in life to define.

How Do You Define Happiness?

Now, let's go back to that difficult question: "what is happiness?"

Have you thought about it already? Let me give you an example of how hard it is to define happiness.

Right now, I'm drinking a cup of coffee while writing the outline of this article about how to define happiness. Am I happy right now? Yes, I'm feeling pretty happy:

- I've got nothing to worry about.
- All my basic needs are met.
- My family, friends, and girlfriend are all happy as well.
- The weather is nice.
- I'm going outside in a couple of minutes to go for a walk.

These things are all making me feel pretty happy right now.

By that logic, let's define my happiness as follows:

"Happiness is when I'm in a worry-free state, the weather is nice, everybody I know is alright and I can enjoy a hot cup of coffee."

Voila. There it is. My definition of happiness.

The keys to my happiness are obvious now,

and I know enough in order to lead the happiest life I can. I just need to focus on the things I listed above.

Wait a second... If it were this simple, then why have I ever been unhappy?

You might have guessed it already, but I made a very simple error. I assumed that what makes me happy today will make me happy for the rest of my life. And that's just wrong.

Happiness is something that not only changes from person to person, but it's also constantly evolving from day to day.

Your definition of happiness changes over time. This is why happiness is such a difficult concept, and why there's not a single "key to happiness".

Whoever tells you otherwise is likely not aware that people change, and that people don't always share the same values, goals, and purposes.

Finding Your Key to True Happiness

So, where to look for true happiness if a single

key to happiness doesn't exist?

Read on to find out...

Define What Happiness Means to You

For a minute, I want you to do consider your own happiness. I want you to think back of last week, and consider what things you did that had a positive effect on your happiness.

What things had a significant influence on your mood? What comes to your mind?

Was it spending time with your friends? Was it a great movie you watched? Did you attend an exciting sports event? Or did you enjoy sipping hot coffee on a sunny Wednesday morning? It could obviously be just about anything!

It's important to realize that all these things were part of your "key to happiness". Your happiness was defined by these things, and you just measured a small part of that.

Does that mean you now know all the answers? Do you now know how to live the rest of your life? No. But you do know what things made you happy last week, and that's very useful information when determining your own definition of happiness to build on.

If you consciously keep track of what factors determine your happiness, then you are more likely to find out just how much your definition of happiness can vary from time to time. This knowledge can help you find your key to happiness.

You see, even though happiness is claimed to be the factor of life that's the most difficult to measure, you can still measure how you define your own happiness each day. It's simple.

For me personally, when I think back of last weekend, I remember that I really enjoyed spending time with my girlfriend, walking through the woods on a sunny day and just relaxing (a.k.a. doing nothing!)

These are happiness factors that were a vital part of my happiness definition this weekend. I had just survived a long and busy week at work, so I was really trying to find some easy enjoyment. The things that I did this weekend were perfect for the occasion, as it was a very happy day for me.

If you were to ask me what the key to my happiness was that weekend, I'd give you the following answer:

To spend quality time with my girlfriend, being able to enjoy the good weather while being carefree and relaxed.

While this is unlikely to be the key to your happiness for the rest of your life, it is a pretty good start.

You can do exactly the same. All you need to do is to define your own happiness from day to day.

Find Your Purpose in Life

The next step to determining your key to happiness is to determine the things that give you purpose. You will live a fulfilling life when you're happily tracking towards a purpose. Something that you're passionate about.

Let's use the previous example of my key to happiness. Will I be happy for the rest of my life when I focus exclusively on a relaxed and carefree feeling? Probably not, because it will not lead to a very fulfilling life. Not for me, at least.

There are some things that drive my actions in a much bigger sense than only my daily, short-term happiness. For some people, that purpose could be:

- To take care of a loving family
- To build a successful company
- To climb the highest mountains
- To be rich and famous

You have to find out what your purpose in life is in order to truly determine your key to happiness. Only then will you be able to define a sustainable plan that will make you both happy and fulfilled.

It's important to know that you can find your purpose only when trying out new things. This is a crucial part of finding your key to happiness. You can't read an article online (like this one) and suddenly learn about what your key to happiness is!

The same thing goes for finding your purpose. You can't expect to find your purpose without trying new things. People stumble upon their purpose in life in lots of different ways.[1]

If you find figuring out your purpose challenging, take a look at this article: How to Find the Purpose of Life and Start Living a Fulfilling Life

Combine Your Purpose in Life with Your Definition on Happiness

Now, this might sound like a mouthful:

A Purpose in Life x Keys to Your Happiness = Fulfilling Life?

It's actually really simple. Let's take the following example:

I've found that my purpose in life is to become the CEO of a great and powerful charity (I know, I know...)

I feel a purpose and sense of accomplishment when working towards these goals. However, should I therefore sacrifice everything in my life in order to reach that purpose? Should I work 100 hours a week, disregard any relationships and use sleep medication just to fall asleep under the stress?

Nope. If I do that, I might reach my purpose, but I won't still be happy.

However, if I spend the rest of my life similar to how I spent my last weekend (enjoying the sun and walking through the forest) I will also miss long-term happiness. That's because I won't feel like my life has a purpose.

Your key to happiness and the purpose of your life need to compliment each other. They need to be in balance.

You've probably heard the saying:

"Happiness is a journey, not a destination". Think of the destination as your purpose, and think of the journey as the things you do that make you happy (the keys to your happiness).

You can't spend your life running (or sprinting) towards your destination, because you'll forget to enjoy the journey. At the same time, you can't head out on your journey without having a destination in mind. That's why I believe **your happiness is a product of both the journey and the destination**.

Or in other words, you need to combine your purpose in life with the keys to your happiness in order to lead a fulfilling life. This will allow you to create a road map – a specific and concise plan – that will help you determine how to best lead your life. If you've done that, you're ready to steer your life in the best direction possible!

How to Be Happy: 16 Ways Backed by Science

1. Do What Brings You Meaning

Our lives may be meaningless, or our goals may be unachievable if we take a closer look at ourselves and our lives. However, having a purposeful intention can help you be happy in life by drawing your focus on the things that are most important to you, such as your loved ones, faith, career, and many other aspects of your life.

It allows you to cut ties with people or activities that aren't aligned with your values. Staying motivated is essential to set and accomplishing short and long-term goals when things get tough.

It also and perhaps most importantly, gives you a sense that your efforts are having a positive impact on the world.

"When a person can't find a deep sense of

meaning, they distract themselves with pleasure." -Viktor Frankly

Many affluent people experience unhappiness despite how much money, respect, or fame they have because of one big reason—meaninglessness. Ultimately, happiness stems from meaning.

2. Add More Exercise to Your Routine

Exercise causes the production of feel-good endorphins, which make you happier after a workout or even just a short trip to the store. I've never encountered somebody unhappy after exercising!

The University of Toronto did a great job and analyzed no less than 25 research studies. The conclusion was that physical activity does help to keep depression at bay.

The best study I'm aware of was one that assigned three groups of depressed people to a regimen of antidepressants, physical activity, or a combination of the two. It is unsurprising that all three groups were happier than before, but did this happiness last?

The exercise-only treatment group had an exceptionally low relapse rate of just 9 percent six months later. However, the other two groups had relapse rates between 38 and 31 percent, meaning that nearly a third of them were once again depressed.

If you find yourself too busy to fit in exercise in your day, try this to get started:

3. Positive Thinking Affects Your Performance

"Happiness is the precursor to success." – Shawn Achor, researcher and author of *The Happiness Advantage: The Seven Principles of Positive Psychology That Fuel Success and Performance at Work*

Seems like a pipe dream? Well, according to author Shawn Achor, you can anticipate 10% of your long-term happiness if you are fully aware of all the variables that influence it. These variables include stressors, hassles, successes, economic conditions, relationships, and so on.

How you interpret the outside world makes up the remaining 90%. With positive thinking, you can attain up to 30% more energy, creativity, and productivity. The key is to think positively today, rather than waiting till you are well-off and well-known.

4. Dump Your Negative Thoughts

Some people struggle greatly to overcome negative thoughts because it overpowers them.

A University of Madrid study found that writing your negative thoughts down on a piece of paper and then destroying it was effective in ridding these thoughts from the mind.[2] They advise you to burn, tear up, or dump the paper in the trash!

Physically getting rid of them does help to lessen their damaging effects. Psychologists advise doing this frequently.

5. Treasure Your Experiences More Than Your Possessions

Thomas Gilovich, a psychologist at Cornell University, has conducted extensive research on why it is preferable to value special memories and enjoyable experiences over the goods we acquire.

There are many reasons for this, as outlined in

his study published in the Journal of Experimental Social Psychology.[3] The initial joy we feel when buying and taking possession of that new automobile, TV, or computer can be destroyed by comparing and looking at better items after purchase.

However, cherishing experiences is not nearly as harmful. They are unique, ours, and they bring us longer-lasting delight. We should always try to travel somewhere new or go hiking.

6. Write Down Why You Are Grateful

Feeling and thinking about things you're grateful for as soon as you wake up is a terrific method to increase happiness.

Research on our brain shows that we tend to always focus on the negative things of life like worries, tragedies, failures, and discontent. Negativity is the default position.

"We've got this negativity bias that's a kind of bug in the stone-age brain in the 21st century." Rick Hanson, neuropsychologist.

That is why it is important to concentrate on

positive things. Specifically to identify our reasons for gratitude. Here are a few concepts on how to achieve this:

- When you wake up in the morning, mentally recite three things for which you are thankful
- Keep the list nearby to remind yourself periodically
- If you want to, use Facebook or Twitter. It's helpful to remind your audience that this genuinely works
- Thank a coworker for assisting with a project or task by calling or buying coffee
- Consider helping someone or volunteering a few hours each week

But is there any scientific proof that this actually works? Check out this link to see some of the numerous studies on gratitude and its many benefits.

7. Practice Mindfulness

What does being mindful_mean? It simply means that you focus on the current moment, give it all your attention, and accept it without judgment. The psychology and medical fields are now seeing a rise in this phenomenon. It can improve mood, lower stress levels, and enhance the quality of life when practiced regularly.

By focusing on the present, you can enjoy good feelings and other bodily sensations like touch and smell. Think about how happy they make you feel. It is quite successful at helping people let go of the past and stop worrying about terrifying possibilities for the future.

8. Don't Forget Your Beauty Sleep

After conducting numerous studies, researchers arrived at the conclusion that lack of sleep greatly increases your tendency to be negative. This particular study is fascinating.

The hippocampus, the area of the brain that processes our happy thoughts, was the focus of the researchers' attention. This function begins to sag, and negative thoughts creep in far more than usual when we are sleep deprived.

Researchers gave sleep-deprived students a list of words to remember to demonstrate this.

When it came to the positive or neutral terms, they were only getting about 31 percent of these accurate. However, they scored highly on all the negative phrases (81 percent). Dr. Robert Stick gold has conducted similar experiments on sleep and memory.[4]

Now you know why people are always in a bad mood when they do not get enough sleep.

9. Dedicate a Little Time to Helping Others

Although it may temporarily improve happiness, buying bigger homes, vehicles, and phones do not have long-term positive impacts on people's overall happiness. It is short-lived.

Researchers have found that when we dedicate a little time or money to helping others, there is a significant effect on our own happiness.[5]

10. Focus on Your Strengths

Are you courageous, curious, or open-minded? How are you utilizing these talents to enhance your and others' lives? These are important questions because people generally are happier when they focus on their strengths rather than their flaws.

One of the best methods for achieving happiness and improving the world is to reach our full potential by making the most of our talents.

11. Let Go of Grudges

Do you know how much mental and physical energy it takes to hold onto a grudge? To get a little idea of this, try to empty your mind of your anger towards people who have hurt you. Do this for only a few seconds, and you'll be able to tell that there's a massive difference in how you feel.

Grudges are heavy and rob you of happiness. Sure, you will always get hurt by some people, with some being so terrible that it's not so easy to forgive and forget. However, you would have to learn how to let go of this no matter what.

That doesn't mean you have to be friends with everyone, especially those who are a threat to you. It only means that you shouldn't hang on to the grudge in your heart so much that it weighs you down. Instead, focus on the possibility of having a much brighter future.

12. Don't Compare Yourself to Others

Many people waltz through life believing that they are competing with others. This stops them from feeling genuinely fulfilled. They begin to think that they can never be enough, and this dissatisfaction wipes the smiles off their faces.[6]

The only person you should compare yourself to is your previous version. That will tell you if you're doing much better or have been in the same spot for a while.

See someone who loves to travel around the world? Suddenly, you're interested in doing that as well, even though you're terrified of flying and constantly uncomfortable when you leave your comfort zone.

That's just you trying to achieve someone else's goals and dreams, not yours. Live at your own pace, knowing precisely what you want.

Remember: You can't achieve true satisfaction when you're always trying to mirror others.

13. Spend Some Time With Good Company

Of course, it's okay to enjoy your company every once in a while. Some alone time is necessary to meditate and listen to yourself. However, this is much different from being a loner.

Even if you don't enjoy being surrounded by many people, you can make the best of this by finding an excellent spot that doesn't choke you up so much. It could be a quiet space at the park where you get to engage in a bit of people-watching.

An even better idea is to hang out with the people who matter to you. Bonding with your loved ones helps you realize that there are still people out there who genuinely care about you and want you happy all the time.

Whether it's planning an adventurous day out with your friends or just simply talking with them, it's much better than spending every single day cooped up indoors all by yourself.

14. Don't Be Materialistic

Materials can be easily destroyed, stolen, or

broken. Thus, holding onto them and becoming emotionally connected to them can never lead to a positive outcome. Avoid being emotionally attached to anything or anyone if you value your own serenity.

According to science and research, those who invest more in materialistic things tend to experience fewer positive emotions and higher levels of anxiety and may fall into substance abuse and depression

It is just like filling up your online shopping basket, thinking the material objects in the cart will bring you happiness, not realizing that they will only provide fleeting pleasure.

15. Create Better Habits

Happiness is a choice you make; it is not a gift from the universe. Rather, it is a state of mind that you cultivate. Making positive life changes can be difficult.

Though it's a long and arduous process, its rewards outweigh its difficulties. We can build a solid foundation for achieving our goals of attaining happiness by cultivating and reinforcing positive habits in our daily lives.

The truth about why it's so hard to break out of old routines is simply the fact that it is a routine; human beings are creatures of habit. Charles Duhigg explains in his book *The Power of Habit* the basic structure of habits consists of a cue (trigger), a routine, and a reward.

For example, stress can be your cue to engage in your routine of smoking a cigarette, which rewards you with a surge of nicotine to relieve your stress.

Duhigg teaches that the key to turning bad habits into good ones is to figure out how to change the routine. Rather than smoking, you can go for a nice walk or meditate to achieve the same stress relief.

If your habits are not making you healthier and happier, that means you may be automatically spending almost half your day doing things that make you unhappy.

16. Get Rid of Negative Emotions with Affirmations

What do you do when negative thoughts creep into your mind? Negative thoughts creeping into your mind will inevitably happen every once in a while, but your response to these thoughts will determine if you can live a happy life.

1. An excellent way to respond to negative thoughts is through words of affirmation. When you practice positive affirmations, it helps in increasing your feelings of self-worth.

You can start each day with words of affirmation. Stand in front of your mirror and repeat sentences like, “I am living my best life” or “I will have an amazing day.”

If you find it challenging to come up with words of affirmation on the spot, write them out the night before. Write at least five positive affirmations that resonate with you and repeat them first thing in the morning.

Bonus: 4 Steps to Stop Fearing Sadness

Pain, sadness, anger, fear, guilt, frustration – they are not to be feared. You should not be scared of negative emotions. They are to be processed, accepted, understood, and moved through to a better emotion.

You don't need to fight your emotions. This 4 step process will help you move from negative emotions to positive ones faster:

Step 1: Hear How You Feel

Don't try to hide from the way you feel. In my experience, clients that do this end up confronting the thing they were hiding from. It tends to be the thing that is holding them back the most.

The difficulty arises when you don't have someone to work with to help you achieve this, and that allows you to keep hiding from what you truly feel.

Step 2: Understand How You Feel

Understanding how you feel can work out *why* you feel that way. Ask yourself the following questions:

- Was there a cause?
- An aggravating factor?
- An emotional vampire?
- An action?

I have a client I started working with last year

who said they dreaded February.

“It goes too fast!” they lamented, adding, “January is too long, and then February flies by, and you feel depressed that the year is going so fast and that you’ve still got so much to do!”

When we worked on this together, they could see how ridiculous this thought was.

If you are lucky enough to live for 70 years, that’s 70 Januarys you will hate — 2,170 days of your life feeling unhappiness. About 8.5% of your life will be sad just because of the name of a month - and that’s before we add February.

The realization that a month helped create an emotion before anything had even happened helped this client appreciate their feelings.

Step 3: Accept It

Acceptance is a huge part of achieving and attaining happiness. It leaves room to move on to the next thing.

Step 4: Ditch It

Seeing a process unfolding before you makes it much quicker to decide to ditch it. Negative feelings are not permanent, and you can move them back to happiness. There's no such thing as a bad emotion, just bad results you get when you hang on to it.

Pain is part of happiness; it's on the opposite end of the scale. Think of all the emotions that are considered negative or bad and ask yourself:

"Can you have one without the other?"

Final Thoughts

These methods are all known to increase happiness, according to science. If you believe that you have too many obligations and that it is too late to live a different life, reconsider! Living a better and more fulfilled life is never too late.

The most important thing to remember when trying to define your keys to a happy and fulfilling life is simple:

There is no universal key that leads to your happiness. That's because your happiness is unique in each and every single way. What you can do is:

- Realize that you can define the factors that make you happy.
- Know that your happiness – and the factors that influence it – change over time, and so will your “key to happiness”.
- Find out what your purpose in life is. You can only do this by trying out many things. You can’t learn this from simple reading an article!
- Combine your purpose and the things that make you happy in order to get the best idea of how to steer your life in the best direction possible

Reference

[1] Psychology Today: 25 Studies Confirm: Exercise Prevents Depression

[2] Universidad Autonomy de Madrid: Treating Thoughts as Material Objects Can Increase or Decrease Their Impact on Evaluation

[3] Journal of Experimental Social Psychology: Spending on experiences versus possessions advances more immediate happiness

[4] Healthy Sleep: Sleep and Memory

[5] News Harvard: Money spent on others can buy happiness

[6] The Brain Lift: Don't Compare Yourself to Others

[7] Greater Good Magazine: How Gratitude Beats Materialism

www.ingramcontent.com/pod-product-compliance
Lightning Source LLC
LaVergne TN
LVHW041305150826
845673LV00008B/2748
* 9 7 9 8 3 6 6 9 1 3 1 6 4 *